GOOD SHIT
BAD SHIT

a journal
for life's
little ups
and downs

Huck & Pucker
Huck Towers
46 West Street
Chichester
West Sussex
PO19 1RP
UK

www.huckandpucker.com

Printed and bound in the Czech Republic

ISBN: 978-1-909865-07-5

Substantial discounts on bulk quantities of Huck & Pucker products are available to corporations, professional associations and other organisations. For details contact Nicky Douglas by telephone: +44 (0) 1243 756902, fax: +44 (0) 1243 786300 or email: huck@huckandpucker.com

This journal belongs to:

....

LIFE IS A
FOUR-LETTER WORD.

Lenny Bruce

Use the two columns to write down the good
and bad shit that happened today

GOOD SHIT   BAD SHIT

. . . .

. . . .

. . . .

. . . .

. . . .

. . . .

. . . .

. . . .

. . . .

. . . .

Sum up the day by shading in the Shit-O-Meter

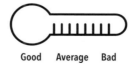

Good   Average   Bad

date. . . . .

**GOOD
SHIT**

Use the box below to draw the
good shit that happened today...

BAD SHIT

...and use the box above to draw the bad shit

date . . . .

Use the two columns to write down the good
and bad shit that happened today

GOOD SHIT   BAD SHIT

. . . .

. . . .

. . . .

. . . .

. . . .

. . . .

. . . .

. . . .

. . . .

. . . .

Sum up the day by shading in the Shit-O-Meter

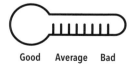

Good   Average   Bad

SCRAP THIS SHIT!

Draw or write some awful shit you'd like to forget in the flame below, cut it out and destroy it forever!

GOOD THINGS COME TO THOSE WHO WAIT.

Proverb

Use the two columns to write down the good
and bad shit that happened today

GOOD SHIT   BAD SHIT

. . . .

. . . .

. . . .

. . . .

. . . .

. . . .

. . . .

. . . .

. . . .

. . . .

Sum up the day by shading in the Shit-O-Meter

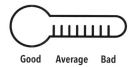

Good   Average   Bad

date. . . . .

BEST SHIT OF THE WEEK

(draw or write in the hand above)

WORST SHIT OF THE WEEK

(draw or write in the hand below)

date. . . . .

Use the two columns to write down the good
and bad shit that happened today

GOOD SHIT   # BAD SHIT

. . . .

. . . .

. . . .

. . . .

. . . .

. . . .

. . . .

. . . .

. . . .

. . . .

Sum up the day by shading in the Shit-O-Meter

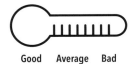

Good   Average   Bad

FRAME THIS SHIT!

Draw or write some amazing shit you'd like to
remember in the rosette below, cut it out and
put it somewhere you can show it off!

date. . . . .

IF, AS WE'RE CONSTANTLY TOLD, THE WORLD IS OUR OYSTER, IT'S DEFINITELY A DODGY ONE.

Damian Barr

**Use the two columns to write down the good
and bad shit that happened today**

GOOD SHIT   BAD SHIT

· · · · · · · · · · · · · · · · · ·   · · · · · · · · · · · · · · · · · ·

· · · · · · · · · · · · · · · · · ·   · · · · · · · · · · · · · · · · · ·

· · · · · · · · · · · · · · · · · ·   · · · · · · · · · · · · · · · · · ·

· · · · · · · · · · · · · · · · · ·   · · · · · · · · · · · · · · · · · ·

· · · · · · · · · · · · · · · · · ·   · · · · · · · · · · · · · · · · · ·

· · · · · · · · · · · · · · · · · ·   · · · · · · · · · · · · · · · · · ·

· · · · · · · · · · · · · · · · · ·   · · · · · · · · · · · · · · · · · ·

· · · · · · · · · · · · · · · · · ·   · · · · · · · · · · · · · · · · · ·

· · · · · · · · · · · · · · · · · ·   · · · · · · · · · · · · · · · · · ·

· · · · · · · · · · · · · · · · · ·   · · · · · · · · · · · · · · · · · ·

Sum up the day by shading in the Shit-O-Meter

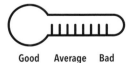

Good   Average   Bad

date. . . . .

Use the box below to draw the good shit that happened today...

...and use the box above to draw the bad shit

date. . . . .

**Use the two columns to write down the good
and bad shit that happened today**

GOOD SHIT   BAD SHIT

. . . .

. . . .

. . . .

. . . .

. . . .

. . . .

. . . .

. . . .

. . . .

Sum up the day by shading in the Shit-O-Meter

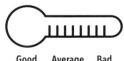

Good   Average   Bad

SCRAP THIS SHIT!

Draw or write some awful shit you'd like to forget in the flame
below, cut it out and destroy it forever!

EVERY MAN IS THE ARCHITECT OF HIS OWN FORTUNE.

Sallust

Use the two columns to write down the good
and bad shit that happened today

GOOD SHIT BAD SHIT

. . . .

. . . .

. . . .

. . . .

. . . .

. . . .

. . . .

. . . .

. . . .

. . . .

Sum up the day by shading in the Shit-O-Meter

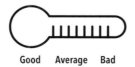

Good   Average   Bad

date. . . . .

BEST SHIT OF THE WEEK

(draw or write in the hand above)

WORST SHIT OF THE WEEK

(draw or write in the hand below)

date. . . . .

Use the two columns to write down the good
and bad shit that happened today

GOOD SHIT

BAD SHIT

. . . .

. . . .

. . . .

. . . .

. . . .

. . . .

. . . .

. . . .

. . . .

. . . .

Sum up the day by shading in the Shit-O-Meter

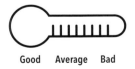

Good   Average   Bad

FRAME THIS SHIT!

Draw or write some amazing shit you'd like to remember in the rosette below, cut it out and put it somewhere you can show it off!

date. . . . .

LIFE IS A SHIT SANDWICH AND EVERY DAY YOU TAKE ANOTHER BITE.

Joe Schmidt

Use the two columns to write down the good
and bad shit that happened today

GOOD SHIT   BAD SHIT

. . . .

. . . .

. . . .

. . . .

. . . .

. . . .

. . . .

. . . .

. . . .

. . . .

Sum up the day by shading in the Shit-O-Meter

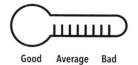

Good   Average   Bad

date..............

Use the box below to draw the good shit that happened today...

GOOD
SHIT

...and use the box above to draw the bad shit

date. . . . .

Use the two columns to write down the good
and bad shit that happened today

GOOD SHIT

BAD SHIT

. . . .
. . . .
. . . .
. . . .
. . . .
. . . .
. . . .
. . . .
. . . .

Sum up the day by shading in the Shit-O-Meter

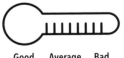

Good   Average   Bad

SCRAP THIS SHIT!

Draw or write some awful shit you'd like to forget in the flame below, cut it out and destroy it forever!

GOOD LUCK BEATS EARLY RISING.

Irish proverb

Use the two columns to write down the good
and bad shit that happened today

GOOD SHIT   BAD SHIT

. . . .

. . . .

. . . .

. . . .

. . . .

. . . .

. . . .

. . . .

. . . .

. . . .

Sum up the day by shading in the Shit-O-Meter

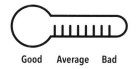

Good   Average   Bad

date. . . . .

BEST SHIT OF THE WEEK

(draw or write in the hand above)

WORST SHIT OF THE WEEK

(draw or write in the hand below)

date. . . . .

Use the two columns to write down the good
and bad shit that happened today

GOOD SHIT   BAD SHIT

. . . .

. . . .

. . . .

. . . .

. . . .

. . . .

. . . .

. . . .

. . . .

. . . .

Sum up the day by shading in the Shit-O-Meter

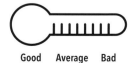

Good   Average   Bad

FRAME THIS SHIT!

Draw or write some amazing shit you'd like to
remember in the rosette below, cut it out and
put it somewhere you can show it off!

date. . . . .

LIVING WITH LIFE IS VERY HARD.

Jeanette Winterson

date. . . . .

Use the two columns to write down the good
and bad shit that happened today

GOOD SHIT

BAD SHIT

. . . .

. . . .

. . . .

. . . .

. . . .

. . . .

. . . .

. . . .

. . . .

. . . .

Sum up the day by shading in the Shit-O-Meter

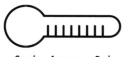

Good   Average   Bad

date. . . . .

**Use the box below to draw the
good shit that happened today...**

...and use the box above to draw the bad shit

date. . . . .

Use the two columns to write down the good
and bad shit that happened today

GOOD SHIT   # BAD SHIT

. . . .　　. . . . .

. . . .　　. . . . .

. . . .　　. . . . .

. . . .　　. . . . .

. . . .　　. . . . .

. . . .　　. . . . .

. . . .　　. . . . .

. . . .　　. . . . .

. . . .　　. . . . .

. . . .　　. . . . .

Sum up the day by shading in the Shit-O-Meter

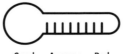

Good　Average　Bad

SCRAP THIS SHIT!

Draw or write some awful shit you'd like to forget in the flame below, cut it out and destroy it forever!

WE ARE PUT ON THIS EARTH TO HAVE A GOOD TIME. THIS MAKES OTHER PEOPLE FEEL GOOD. AND THE CYCLE CONTINUES.

Wolfman Jack

Use the two columns to write down the good
and bad shit that happened today

GOOD SHIT   BAD SHIT

. . . . | . . . .

. . . . | . . . .

. . . . | . . . .

. . . . | . . . .

. . . . | . . . .

. . . . | . . . .

. . . . | . . . .

. . . . | . . . .

. . . . | . . . .

. . . . | . . . .

Sum up the day by shading in the Shit-O-Meter

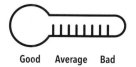

Good   Average   Bad

date. . . . .

BEST SHIT OF THE WEEK

(draw or write in the hand above)

WORST SHIT OF THE WEEK

(draw or write in the hand below)

date. . . . .

Use the two columns to write down the good
and bad shit that happened today

GOOD SHIT

BAD SHIT

. . . .

. . . .

. . . .

. . . .

. . . .

. . . .

. . . .

. . . .

. . . .

. . . .

Sum up the day by shading in the Shit-O-Meter

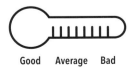

Good   Average   Bad

FRAME THIS SHIT!

Draw or write some amazing shit you'd like to
remember in the rosette below, cut it out and
put it somewhere you can show it off!

date. . . . .

THERE ARE DAYS WHEN IT TAKES ALL YOU'VE GOT JUST TO KEEP UP WITH THE LOSERS.

Robert Orben

Use the two columns to write down the good
and bad shit that happened today

GOOD SHIT   BAD SHIT

. . . .

. . . .

. . . .

. . . .

. . . .

. . . .

. . . .

. . . .

. . . .

. . . .

Sum up the day by shading in the Shit-O-Meter

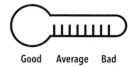

Good   Average   Bad

date. . . . .

**Use the box below to draw the
good shit that happened today...**

GOOD
SHIT

BAD
SHIT

...and use the box above to draw the bad shit

date. . . . .

Use the two columns to write down the good
and bad shit that happened today

GOOD SHIT

BAD SHIT

. . . .

. . . .

. . . .

. . . .

. . . .

. . . .

. . . .

. . . .

. . . .

. . . .

Sum up the day by shading in the Shit-O-Meter

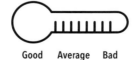

Good   Average   Bad

SCRAP THIS SHIT!

Draw or write some awful shit you'd like to forget in the flame below, cut it out and destroy it forever!

WHEN YOU LOOK UP,
YOU GO UP.

Herschel Walker

date. . . . .

Use the two columns to write down the good
and bad shit that happened today

GOOD SHIT   # BAD SHIT

. . . .

. . . .

. . . .

. . . .

. . . .

. . . .

. . . .

. . . .

. . . .

. . . .

Sum up the day by shading in the Shit-O-Meter

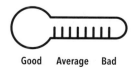

Good   Average   Bad

date. . . . .

BEST SHIT OF THE WEEK

(draw or write in the hand above)

WORST SHIT OF THE WEEK

(draw or write in the hand below)

date. . . . .

Use the two columns to write down the good
and bad shit that happened today

GOOD SHIT   BAD SHIT

. . . .

. . . .

. . . .

. . . .

. . . .

. . . .

. . . .

. . . .

. . . .

. . . .

Sum up the day by shading in the Shit-O-Meter

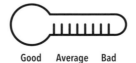

Good   Average   Bad

FRAME THIS SHIT!

Draw or write some amazing shit you'd like to
remember in the rosette below, cut it out and
put it somewhere you can show it off!

date. . . . .

I AM ANGRY NEARLY EVERY DAY OF MY LIFE.

Louisa May Alcott

Use the two columns to write down the good
and bad shit that happened today

GOOD SHIT BAD SHIT

. . . .

. . . .

. . . .

. . . .

. . . .

. . . .

. . . .

. . . .

. . . .

. . . .

Sum up the day by shading in the Shit-O-Meter

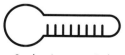

Good   Average   Bad

date. . . . .

GOOD SHIT

Use the box below to draw the
good shit that happened today...

...and use the box above to draw the bad shit

date. . . . .

**Use the two columns to write down the good
and bad shit that happened today**

GOOD SHIT   BAD SHIT

. . . .

. . . .

. . . .

. . . .

. . . .

. . . .

. . . .

. . . .

. . . .

. . . .

Sum up the day by shading in the Shit-O-Meter

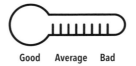

Good   Average   Bad

SCRAP THIS SHIT!

Draw or write some awful shit you'd like to forget in the flame below, cut it out and destroy it forever!

BEFORE YOU CAN BE OLD AND WISE, FIRST YOU HAVE TO BE YOUNG AND STUPID.

Anonymous

Use the two columns to write down the good
and bad shit that happened today

GOOD SHIT   BAD SHIT

. . . .

. . . .

. . . .

. . . .

. . . .

. . . .

. . . .

. . . .

. . . .

. . . .

Sum up the day by shading in the Shit-O-Meter

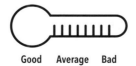

Good   Average   Bad

date..............

BEST SHIT OF THE WEEK

(draw or write in the hand above)

WORST SHIT OF THE WEEK

(draw or write in the hand below)

date. . . . .

Use the two columns to write down the good
and bad shit that happened today

GOOD SHIT   # BAD SHIT

. . . .

. . . .

. . . .

. . . .

. . . .

. . . .

. . . .

. . . .

. . . .

. . . .

Sum up the day by shading in the Shit-O-Meter

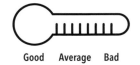

Good   Average   Bad

FRAME THIS SHIT!

Draw or write some amazing shit you'd like to
remember in the rosette below, cut it out and
put it somewhere you can show it off!

date. . . . .

LIFE IS MERELY TERRIBLE.

Franz Kafka

Use the two columns to write down the good
and bad shit that happened today

GOOD SHIT   # BAD SHIT

. . . .

. . . .

. . . .

. . . .

. . . .

. . . .

. . . .

. . . .

. . . .

. . . .

Sum up the day by shading in the Shit-O-Meter

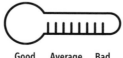

Good   Average   Bad

date. . . . .

**Use the box below to draw the
good shit that happened today...**

GOOD
SHIT

...and use the box above to draw the bad shit

date. . . . .

Use the two columns to write down the good
and bad shit that happened today

GOOD SHIT

BAD SHIT

. . . .　. . . . .

. . . .　. . . . .

. . . .　. . . . .

. . . .　. . . . .

. . . .　. . . . .

. . . .　. . . . .

. . . .　. . . . .

. . . .　. . . . .

. . . .　. . . . .

. . . .　. . . . .

Sum up the day by shading in the Shit-O-Meter

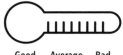

Good　Average　Bad

SCRAP THIS SHIT!

Draw or write some awful shit you'd like to forget in the flame below, cut it out and destroy it forever!

THE WAY I SEE IT, YOU SHOULD LIVE EVERY DAY LIKE IT'S YOUR BIRTHDAY.

Paris Hilton

Use the two columns to write down the good
and bad shit that happened today

GOOD SHIT   BAD SHIT

. . . .

. . . .

. . . .

. . . .

. . . .

. . . .

. . . .

. . . .

. . . .

. . . .

Sum up the day by shading in the Shit-O-Meter

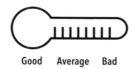

Good   Average   Bad

date. . . . .

BEST SHIT OF THE WEEK

(draw or write in the hand above)

WORST SHIT OF THE WEEK

(draw or write in the hand below)

date. . . . .

**Use the two columns to write down the good
and bad shit that happened today**

GOOD SHIT   BAD SHIT

. . . .

. . . .

. . . .

. . . .

. . . .

. . . .

. . . .

. . . .

. . . .

. . . .

Sum up the day by shading in the Shit-O-Meter

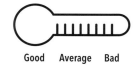

Good   Average   Bad

FRAME THIS SHIT!

Draw or write some amazing shit you'd like to
remember in the rosette below, cut it out and
put it somewhere you can show it off!

date. . . . .

SOMETIMES YOU CAN GET A SPLINTER EVEN SLIDING DOWN A RAINBOW.

Terri Guillemets

date. . . . .

Use the two columns to write down the good
and bad shit that happened today

GOOD SHIT   BAD SHIT

. . . .

. . . .

. . . .

. . . .

. . . .

. . . .

. . . .

. . . .

. . . .

. . . .

Sum up the day by shading in the Shit-O-Meter

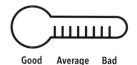

Good   Average   Bad

date. . . . .

GOOD SHIT

Use the box below to draw the good shit that happened today...

...and use the box above to draw the bad shit

date. . . . .

Use the two columns to write down the good
and bad shit that happened today

GOOD SHIT   BAD SHIT

. . . .

. . . .

. . . .

. . . .

. . . .

. . . .

. . . .

. . . .

. . . .

. . . .

Sum up the day by shading in the Shit-O-Meter

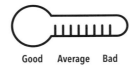

Good   Average   Bad

SCRAP THIS SHIT!

Draw or write some awful shit you'd like to forget in the flame below, cut it out and destroy it forever!

MOST FOLKS ARE AS HAPPY AS THEY MAKE UP THEIR MINDS TO BE.

Abraham Lincoln

Use the two columns to write down the good
and bad shit that happened today

GOOD SHIT   BAD SHIT

. . . . | . . . .

. . . . | . . . .

. . . . | . . . .

. . . . | . . . .

. . . . | . . . .

. . . . | . . . .

. . . . | . . . .

. . . . | . . . .

. . . . | . . . .

Sum up the day by shading in the Shit-O-Meter

Good   Average   Bad

date. . . . .

BEST SHIT OF THE WEEK

(draw or write in the hand above)

WORST SHIT OF THE WEEK

(draw or write in the hand below)

date. . . . .

Use the two columns to write down the good
and bad shit that happened today

GOOD SHIT　　BAD SHIT

. . . .　　. . . . .

. . . .　　. . . . .

. . . .　　. . . . .

. . . .　　. . . . .

. . . .　　. . . . .

. . . .　　. . . . .

. . . .　　. . . . .

. . . .　　. . . . .

. . . .　　. . . . .

. . . .　　. . . . .

Sum up the day by shading in the Shit-O-Meter

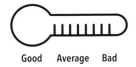

Good　　Average　　Bad

FRAME THIS SHIT!

Draw or write some amazing shit you'd like to
remember in the rosette below, cut it out and
put it somewhere you can show it off!

date. . . . .

NINETY PER CENT OF EVERYTHING IS CRAP.

Theodore Sturgeon

Use the two columns to write down the good
and bad shit that happened today

GOOD SHIT   BAD SHIT

. . . .

. . . .

. . . .

. . . .

. . . .

. . . .

. . . .

. . . .

. . . .

. . . .

Sum up the day by shading in the Shit-O-Meter

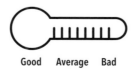

Good   Average   Bad

date. . . . .

Use the box below to draw the
good shit that happened today...

...and use the box above to draw the bad shit

date. . . . .

**Use the two columns to write down the good
and bad shit that happened today**

GOOD SHIT   BAD SHIT

. . . .

. . . .

. . . .

. . . .

. . . .

. . . .

. . . .

. . . .

. . . .

. . . .

Sum up the day by shading in the Shit-O-Meter

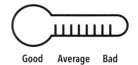

Good   Average   Bad

SCRAP THIS SHIT!

Draw or write some awful shit you'd like to forget in the flame below, cut it out and destroy it forever!

FUN IS GOOD.

Dr Seuss

Use the two columns to write down the good
and bad shit that happened today

GOOD SHIT   # BAD SHIT

. . . .

. . . .

. . . .

. . . .

. . . .

. . . .

. . . .

. . . .

. . . .

. . . .

Sum up the day by shading in the Shit-O-Meter

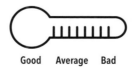

Good   Average   Bad

date. . . . .

BEST SHIT OF THE WEEK

(draw or write in the hand above)

WORST SHIT OF THE WEEK

(draw or write in the hand below)

date . . . .

Use the two columns to write down the good
and bad shit that happened today

GOOD SHIT   BAD SHIT

. . . .

. . . .

. . . .

. . . .

. . . .

. . . .

. . . .

. . . .

. . . .

. . . .

Sum up the day by shading in the Shit-O-Meter

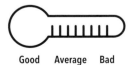

Good   Average   Bad

FRAME THIS SHIT!

Draw or write some amazing shit you'd like to remember in the rosette below, cut it out and put it somewhere you can show it off!

date. . . . .

ISN'T HUMANITY NEAT?
BULLSHIT. WE'RE A VIRUS
WITH SHOES, OK?

Bill Hicks

date. . . . .

Use the two columns to write down the good
and bad shit that happened today

GOOD SHIT   BAD SHIT

. . . .

. . . .

. . . .

. . . .

. . . .

. . . .

. . . .

. . . .

. . . .

. . . .

Sum up the day by shading in the Shit-O-Meter

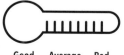

Good   Average   Bad

date. . . . .

Use the box below to draw the
good shit that happened today...

GOOD
SHIT

...and use the box above to draw the bad shit

date. . . . .

Use the two columns to write down the good
and bad shit that happened today

GOOD SHIT   # BAD SHIT

. . . .

. . . .

. . . .

. . . .

. . . .

. . . .

. . . .

. . . .

. . . .

. . . .

Sum up the day by shading in the Shit-O-Meter

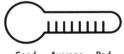

Good   Average   Bad

SCRAP THIS SHIT!

Draw or write some awful shit you'd like to forget in the flame below, cut it out and destroy it forever!

YESTERDAY IS HISTORY, TOMORROW IS A MYSTERY, BUT TODAY IS A GIFT.

Eleanor Roosevelt

Use the two columns to write down the good
and bad shit that happened today

GOOD SHIT   BAD SHIT

. . . .

. . . .

. . . .

. . . .

. . . .

. . . .

. . . .

. . . .

. . . .

. . . .

Sum up the day by shading in the Shit-O-Meter

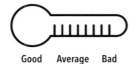

Good   Average   Bad

BEST SHIT OF THE WEEK

(draw or write in the hand above)

WORST SHIT OF THE WEEK

(draw or write in the hand below)

date. . . . .

Use the two columns to write down the good and bad shit that happened today

GOOD SHIT   BAD SHIT

. . . .

. . . .

. . . .

. . . .

. . . .

. . . .

. . . .

. . . .

. . . .

. . . .

Sum up the day by shading in the Shit-O-Meter

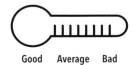

Good   Average   Bad

FRAME THIS SHIT!

Draw or write some amazing shit you'd like to
remember in the rosette below, cut it out and
put it somewhere you can show it off!

date. . . . .

WHEN ILL LUCK BEGINS, IT DOES NOT COME IN SPRINKLES, BUT IN SHOWERS.

Mark Twain

Use the two columns to write down the good
and bad shit that happened today

GOOD SHIT   BAD SHIT

. . . .

. . . .

. . . .

. . . .

. . . .

. . . .

. . . .

. . . .

. . . .

. . . .

Sum up the day by shading in the Shit-O-Meter

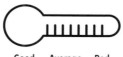

Good   Average   Bad

date. . . . .

Use the box below to draw the
good shit that happened today...

GOOD
SHIT

...and use the box above to draw the bad shit

date. . . . .

**Use the two columns to write down the good
and bad shit that happened today**

GOOD SHIT   BAD SHIT

. . . .

. . . .

. . . .

. . . .

. . . .

. . . .

. . . .

. . . .

. . . .

. . . .

Sum up the day by shading in the Shit-O-Meter

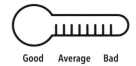

Good   Average   Bad

SCRAP THIS SHIT!

Draw or write some awful shit you'd like to forget in the flame below, cut it out and destroy it forever!

FORTUNE CONVERTS EVERYTHING TO THE ADVANTAGE OF HER FAVOURITES.

François de La Rochefoucauld

Use the two columns to write down the good
and bad shit that happened today

GOOD SHIT　　BAD SHIT

. . . .

. . . .

. . . .

. . . .

. . . .

. . . .

. . . .

. . . .

. . . .

Sum up the day by shading in the Shit-O-Meter

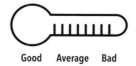

Good   Average   Bad

date. . . . .

BEST SHIT OF THE WEEK

(draw or write in the hand above)

WORST SHIT OF THE WEEK

(draw or write in the hand below)

date. . . . .

Use the two columns to write down the good
and bad shit that happened today

GOOD SHIT

BAD SHIT

. . . .

. . . .

. . . .

. . . .

. . . .

. . . .

. . . .

. . . .

. . . .

. . . .

Sum up the day by shading in the Shit-O-Meter

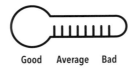

Good   Average   Bad

FRAME THIS SHIT!

Draw or write some amazing shit you'd like to remember in the rosette below, cut it out and put it somewhere you can show it off!

date. . . . .

THE FIRST HUMAN WHO HURLED AN INSULT INSTEAD OF A STONE WAS THE FOUNDER OF CIVILISATION.

Sigmund Freud

date. . . . .

Use the two columns to write down the good
and bad shit that happened today

GOOD SHIT BAD SHIT

. . . .

. . . .

. . . .

. . . .

. . . .

. . . .

. . . .

. . . .

. . . .

. . . .

Sum up the day by shading in the Shit-O-Meter

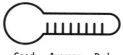

Good   Average   Bad

date. . . . .

GOOD SHIT

Use the box below to draw the good shit that happened today...

...and use the box above to draw the bad shit

date. . . . .

Use the two columns to write down the good
and bad shit that happened today

GOOD SHIT   BAD SHIT

. . . .

. . . .

. . . .

. . . .

. . . .

. . . .

. . . .

. . . .

. . . .

. . . .

Sum up the day by shading in the Shit-O-Meter

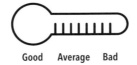

Good   Average   Bad

SCRAP THIS SHIT!

Draw or write some awful shit you'd like to forget in the flame below, cut it out and destroy it forever!

BE HAPPY. IT'S ONE WAY OF BEING WISE.

Colette

date. . . . .

Use the two columns to write down the good
and bad shit that happened today

GOOD SHIT   # BAD SHIT

. . . .

. . . .

. . . .

. . . .

. . . .

. . . .

. . . .

. . . .

. . . .

. . . .

Sum up the day by shading in the Shit-O-Meter

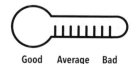

Good   Average   Bad

date. . . . .

BEST SHIT OF THE WEEK

(draw or write in the hand above)

WORST SHIT OF THE WEEK

(draw or write in the hand below)

date . . . .

**Use the two columns to write down the good
and bad shit that happened today**

GOOD SHIT BAD SHIT

. . . .

. . . .

. . . .

. . . .

. . . .

. . . .

. . . .

. . . .

. . . .

. . . .

Sum up the day by shading in the Shit-O-Meter

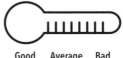

Good   Average   Bad

FRAME THIS SHIT!

Draw or write some amazing shit you'd like to remember in the rosette below, cut it out and put it somewhere you can show it off!

date. . . . .

SHIT HAPPENS.

American proverb

Use the two columns to write down the good
and bad shit that happened today

GOOD SHIT   BAD SHIT

. . . .

. . . .

. . . .

. . . .

. . . .

. . . .

. . . .

. . . .

. . . .

. . . .

Sum up the day by shading in the Shit-O-Meter

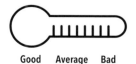

Good   Average   Bad

date. . . . .

GOOD SHIT

Use the box below to draw the
good shit that happened today...

...and use the box above to draw the bad shit

date. . . . .

Use the two columns to write down the good
and bad shit that happened today

GOOD SHIT   # BAD SHIT

. . . .

. . . .

. . . .

. . . .

. . . .

. . . .

. . . .

. . . .

. . . .

. . . .

Sum up the day by shading in the Shit-O-Meter

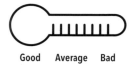

Good   Average   Bad